MW00490124

ZEN
AND THE ART
OF MAKING
A
MORRIS
CHAIR

*Meet your creative spirit
on a path to self-discovery*

AWAKEN CREATIVE POTENTIAL

RANDY GAFNER

KITSAP PUBLISHING

Zen and the Art of Making a Morris Chair
Second edition, published 2016

By Randy Gafner
Cover Design: Morgan Michels
Editing: Cynthia Kane
Craft Examples and Photography: Randy Gafner
Pillow Design Courtesy of: Dianne Ayres
Author Photo: Jason Allen

ISBN: 978-1-942661-31-3

DISCLAIMER
No part of this publication may be reproduced or transmitted in any form or by any means, mechanical or electronic, including photocopying or recording, or by any information storage and retrieval system, or transmitted by email without permission in writing from the author.

Neither the author nor the publisher assumes any responsibility for errors, omissions, or contrary interpretations of the subject matter herein. Any perceived slight of any individual or organization is purely unintentional. Brand and product names are trademarks or registered trademarks of their respective owners.

Creative effort in any form will involve unforeseen levels of risk, including disfigurement, permanent impairment and in rare cases, loss of life. Woodworking, by its nature, requires close contact with sharp tools and powerful motorized cutting and shaping equipment that can, at any time, quickly injure, maim or kill you or those around you. Woodworking, by its nature, often creates noxious dust, dangerous vapors and high levels of dangerous noise.

The author asks you to please observe all posted and implied safety warnings on all equipment, to never operate hand or motorized tools under the influence of psychoactive drugs or alcohol and to leave safety guards on all equipment to protect yourself and those nearby. Always wear ear, eye and breathing protection as necessary and appropriate.

As in most things, you are on your own.

Published by Kitsap Publishing
P.O. Box 1269
Poulsbo, WA 98370
www.KitsapPublishing.com

Printed in the United States of America

TD 20161116

100-10 9 8 7 6 5 4 3 2

Advance Praise

Enjoyed! An elegy to loss, recovery, creativity, and fearlessness--and chairs!

– **Susan Piver** is a Buddhist teacher, a student of Sakyong Mipham Rinpoche and the New York Times bestselling author of 8 books, most recently ***Start Here Now*** on Shambhala.

This concise, lyrical book is much more than a 'how to' manual for building a piece of furniture, but the record of a heartfelt quest for authenticity in the whole personality. It is full of vital lessons on reclaiming our humanity from the ruling culture of artless fakery, and will benefit anyone who is serious about creative endeavor. You might even be inspired to build a chair.

– **James Howard Kunstler** – author of the ***World Made By Hand*** novels and many other books.

The manual for challenging yourself to a creative triumph wrapped in the story of one's man's journey to self-love.

– **Susan Bratton** – Relationship Expert, Personal Life Media. Inc.

Randy offers us an excellent view into the maker's world, describing many things I have experienced but have never seen put into words. He helps dispel the fear of the unknown or at least instructs us that it is perfectly normal to experience it. He also gives us tools to overcome the various roadblocks in the maker's path. This is an instructive and enjoyable book for anyone who creates objects.

– **Dianne Ayres** – Arts & Crafts Period Textiles. www.TextileStudio.com

Randall uses the building of his Morris Chair as a metaphor for the building of a plan for your life. While the woodworker and Arts and Crafts devotee will find his workshop experience laced with insightful details, anyone without any woodworking experience or any association with the Arts and Crafts movement will come away inspired to utilize Randall's insight to craft their own personal identity.

– **Bruce Johnson** – Author, Columnist and Director of the National Arts & Crafts Conference at The Grove Park Inn since 1988

Using the metaphor of constructing a Morris Chair, Randy invites you to journey with him as he carefully articulates life-changing discoveries, each one offering a vision of new life.

– **Donald G. Tritt, Ph.D.** – Emeritus Professor of Psychology, Denison University

There is a deep satisfaction in making something with your own two hands. In "Zen and the Art of Making a Morris Chair," Randy Gafner spends a year building a beautiful chair. Along the way, he makes a few mistakes, learns a great deal about tools and woodworking and gets to know himself a little better. He also discovers and shares many simple and eternal truths.

In our busy lives where our work often does not produce something tangible, there is a lot to be learned and enjoyed by making something. Maybe it's a Morris Chair, maybe it's a loaf of artisanal bread or a hand-knit sweater. The sheer degree of concentration these activities demand alone is a centering exercise to calm the jitters induced by this multitasking world of ours. Making something also offers us a chance for creativity and achievement in a whole new realm that may change the way we view ourselves.

Take the journey with Randy and you just may be inspired to embark on one of your own.

– **Melody Kimmel** – SVP & Partner, Director of Communications Training at FleishmanHillard International Communications, Inc.

It's an engaging read with some great life lessons experienced by Randy Gafner while making an iconic chair from the Arts and Crafts movement. His take struck a chord with me as a novice maker of metal objects. I went through a similar process with all the fear, self doubt, set backs, satisfaction, overreach, community building, and sense of accomplishment. You definitely learn about yourself in attempting to make something of substance with challenging materials and techniques. As you create you make yourself with all the vulnerability implicit in the process and there's no place to hide - your creation is out there for everyone, including yourself to see. A bit scary, lots of fun, leaving you thirsty for more.

– **Franco Ruffini** – retired historic preservation officer and metal fabricator

A mid-19th century artist [William Morris] whose back-to-the basics philosophy influenced a later generation of Arts and Crafts artists and will continue to inspire... "Zen and the Art of Making a Morris Chair" is one chair and one voice but infinite journeys!"

– **Christine Pfister** – Director & Owner of Pentimenti Gallery in Philadelphia. www.pentimenti.com

Dedication

To my Dad the original maker
To my Mom who upheld my curiosity
To my friends who wondered what would be next
To my dreams that do not fail me
To my hands that make real my thoughts

The lyf so short, the craft so long to lern.
- Geoffrey Chaucer (1343-1400 CE)

Ars longa, vita brevis.
Art is long, life is short.

Table of Contents

What I Know

This is a wooden chair with leather upholstery that took me 12 months to build. The chair is made in the American Arts and Crafts Movement design style, popular in the United States 100 years ago.

What I Didn't Know

At the start – Making baby steps on this maker path I did not expect that I would encounter underlying truths from the chair that I would later acknowledge for myself and share with others. My chair making effort began as I rose, like the mythical phoenix bird, from the ashes to start anew and then became a mirror for self--reflection and meditative focus. This became important work for me. This work can become discovery for you.

In the middle – Along the way I didn't expect to find that while making the chair I was also scraping at the bedrock of my inner character. Scraping bedrock? Inner character? Catching my breath in a moment of lucidity my admission of this seems to me a ridiculously improbable statement! Although, in review, making the chair had become like the tip of the iceberg floating above the waves hinting of self-knowledge below the waterline that I can choose to accept or deny, to remember or forget. What happens when you are a maker of things?

At the end – When I sit in the chair I sit with an old friend who was actually in the journey with me, at every step along the way. As we sit together we compare notes as we ponder on many levels: sometimes deep, occasionally sublime. I realize that for some readers my insights gleaned from making this chair will not be new and are not groundbreaking. I accept that. These observations have been available to Homo sapiens faber (making humans) for millennia. Humans making to survive. Humans making to thrive. I bring you this story to encourage you to embrace the change, face the fear, accept the path, discern the choice, and believe in your work.

Make it your way !!!

◆ ◆ ◆

From the Beginning

In the waning months of my marriage, it was difficult to discuss our separation without yelling. So we agreed to meet in a public library where we had to be civil.

That day in autumn 1997, as I sat in the periodical section waiting for my estranged wife to arrive, I was beaten down and tired from months of wrangling. I was ready for a change. From the overstuffed club style library seat in the reading room, I gazed to my left and spied a magazine cover that virtually called out to me from across the room. "Arts and Crafts Furniture That You Can Build," read the cover page of the November 1997 issue of *Popular Mechanics* magazine. In a breathless instant I was intrigued. Sure, I had built a few things before, but I had never thought looking at the pictures that I could build furniture. But what if I could? How would I do it? Where would I do it? What would I make? The questions came fast, while the answers came slowly.

At the time of my separation, my investment dream of sweat equity in a "livable shell" rowhouse in a "frontier" neighborhood of North-west Washington, DC had become a nightmare, imprisoned by crack dealers on the corners and gunfire in the streets. My personal hell began with a misfired pistol to my forehead and the command from a street thug to "give it up." I thought I was done, the pistol clicked once either unloaded or a misfire. He took my wallet and I ran. This event became the on-ramp to a slippery road where, in a span of mere months, I lost my house, my spouse and my job.

I felt like I had hit bottom there at the library as I waited to meet my estranged wife to once again comb through the ashes of our failed marriage. Stunned by total financial loss and with my personal identity in shreds, this idea of building furniture seemed like a way out of the darkness. By making my own furniture from the plans in the magazine, I felt that this could somehow help me re-claim my life.

My interest in American Arts and Crafts Furniture started early when I was a baby. My grandparents had been given a Drop Arm Settle, made by the J. M. Young Furniture Company in Camden, New York as a wedding gift.

This fumed oak[1], minimally upholstered drop arm settle was always in my grandmother's living room at the farmhouse where it stood stoically for years, its back against the wall. When it was naptime for any of her visiting 20 infant grandchildren, the set-

tle was turned to face the wall to create a makeshift crib. I napped in this drop arm settle as a baby.

As I grew older and could stand by the settle, the through-tenons on the arms, shaped like pyramids, were intriguing to my little hands.

Later, as a young man, I noticed how the exposed oak pins secured the steam-bent seat back to the seat upright, similar to other furniture made in central New York State in the early 1900s.

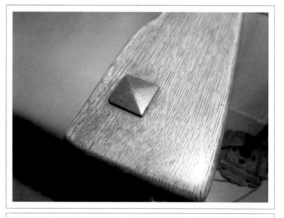

Then as I went off to college, I forgot about my grandparent's furniture with its quartersawn, ray flake[2] highlights, wood grain and exposed joinery that elegantly revealed the method of construction. For the novice, there appear to be no secrets in

Arts and Crafts furniture. For the devotee, there are many.

This settle and another piece at my grandparents' home, a fumed white oak library table, were my first introduction to Arts and Crafts Movement furniture. They were designed and built in a small factory in New York State during a time of social transition from the overly ornate Victorian period at the close of the 19th century to a period of progressive reform in the early 20th Century. The idealism of the Movement flourished in those decades, and continued until the opening salvos of the First World War in 1914. In that time, people were encouraged to craft and build for themselves. The iconic *Popular Mechanics* magazine started during this time period, in 1902, and published do-it-yourself (DIY) plans of Arts and Crafts furniture that you could build. Sears and Roebuck & Company and The Aladdin Company designed kits of entire houses that you could buy and construct on your lot using your skills and tools. Manual training -- wood shop, metal shop and home economics classes -- entered the curriculum of public

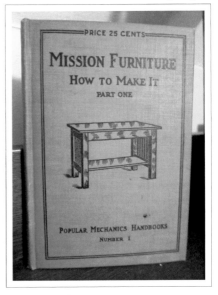

schools in the early 1900s. The *Craftsman Magazine*, published by furniture maker Gustav Stickley, contained architectural plans for homes built in the Arts and Crafts style. *The Craftsman* also published plans for DIY furniture that the readers could build to put in their Craftsman-style homes.

A century later, in the 21st century, these ideals of crafting, building, and making our own things are a challenge. In the not too distant past, your hands would have made your own tools, or made your own clothes, or kneaded your own bread. Were there benefits and life lessons learned by those toolmakers and builders? You bet there were. These were the skills that guaranteed survival for the social group.

In this increasingly technological age, someone else designs the devices and stuff of our lives, and it is impersonally built for us. Because of this, we don't gain possible life lessons and personal insights by applying head, heart and hands to the creation effort.

In this book, I want to show you not only how to approach DIY projects, but also to highlight the life lessons that you can learn from them. Here I share with you how building a Drop Arm Spindle Side Morris Chair taught me how to welcome change, overcome fear, let go of judgment, make choices, and finally, how to believe in myself.

◆ ◆ ◆

CHAPTER 1

Metamorphosis

Something ventured, something gained. That's a different twist on an old saying about motivation. As you take on that new resolve to start patching and painting your drywall or other DIY projects, you may encounter shifts and changes. When we take risks we learn more about our own and others' behavior, how to set realistic expectations, and how to cultivate patience.

Your Behavior and Others' Behavior

Your choice to create for yourself can be a very exciting ride that leads you to a more fulfilled life of opportunities and challenges. At the least, you will start something anew that you've not tried before. But watch out! With a thread of humor woven through this caution, your willingness for DIY expression might change your behavior and might require a change for others.

◆ ◆ ◆

What you change about yourself might change the way that other people perceive you.

◆ ◆ ◆

This active change in your behavior could be disruptive for your friends and family who've known you from times before. They might question your motives in this new adventure. They might be threatened by your audacity to move on without their permission. They might ask you to consider your responsibilities to them or to others in your care.

I would ask you to assess your resolve and dedication to your new creative pursuit and then once decided, move with all haste, as you can, to take steps toward your goal.

In my case, I was resolved to start and complete my chair. For quite some time I had admired and wanted a Morris Chair. But I was in a bind. The original antique models are rare and expensive. The reproduction models are nice but lacked the handcrafted look that I desired. When I found a local woodshop where I could build the chair, I gathered my plans and wood, impatient to start. I was going to build my Morris Chair in a public workshop in Arlington County, Virgina. As I studied the chair plan books, I became excited about making ways to really make this chair my own. I felt as though I could do this. I felt as though I was prepared. For much of my life, I had been learning about tools and tool safety. Soon after I started working on the project in the shop, I quickly became the "Chair Guy."

At the time, I was living and breathing chair design and construction, so this was a logical name that seemed to stick. Everyone could see my dedication to the effort as I showed up on Wednesday evening and Saturday afternoons to work on my projects. As the people around you learn about your emerging DIY interests, they might change the names that they call you.

Some people are going to offer you their genuine support as they live vicariously through your experience. They might not have the personal bravery to move ahead to address their own DIY interests as you do, but I hope that they support you in your efforts to better yourself. They might not even be aware of their own latent, yet slumbering desires to change their lives with their own DIY efforts.

You might become very popular. Are you going to welcome the requests from others who will be asking you for advice on their languishing projects? You might start getting requests for advice on fixing water leaks in your friends' basements. They might stop you on the street to ask you about yarn selection for their mittens or whether you prefer heirloom tomatoes to the modern hybrids. Still others might be threatened by your efforts as they begin to assess themselves in light of your enlightened choice to become more than what they've known you for.

What would happen to your social standing if you started to mix and make your own fresh pasta? The concept of having friends over for dinner changes when you serve your own rolled out fresh linguine. Your relational dynamics would be at risk to change. Watch for it.

Know that there will be changes.

Setting Realistic Expectations

What about the risk of picking a "first time" creative goal that is too complex or too rigorous? Nobody likes being over their head as they swim in uncharted waters. What could happen?

◆ ◆ ◆

Carefully balance your actual and imagined skills with the emerging challenge before you.

◆ ◆ ◆

Perhaps you decide to garden a large plot, and your daily schedule changes and you can't manage the weeds or the animal and insect pests overwhelm you? Maybe you'll be tempted to make a complex dessert for the important Saturday afternoon dinner party. Better not if you are still developing the skills to boil water to make oat-meal. Please know that there is a scale of difficulty for all of your DIY projects. Start with small efforts and then scale up appropriately to larger ones. Carefully consider and realistically assess your abilities.

When you start with too great a challenge, there is a danger that you might get stalled and just give up part way into the process because your project is not giving you the immediate satisfaction that you need to feel good about your choice. I confess to you, this Morris Chair was not the first fine furniture project I had built. Novice woodworkers who see a picture of the iconic chair declare that the Morris Chair is what they want to make before they've ever picked up a wood chisel. I suggest to them that they instead start with the picture frame.

What you need to know for the Morris Chair, you can learn from building the picture frame. With the frame you can learn about mortises, tenons and the design value of a shadow caused by different thicknesses of oak. Start with the simple, move to the complex.

Too ambitious, too rigorous, too soon? My first project in the Arts and Crafts style was an overly complex pyramid lampshade with mica shellac diffusion. Appearing simple in design, the shade geometry and precision joinery required more than 3 months to design and construct.

In reviewing my experience with the shade, I must admit that the shade was very exciting to build but it did test the limits of my woodworking knowledge at the time.

Midway through lampshade making, I realized that I had taken on

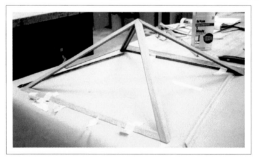

this project too early in my shop experience. To naively add to the challenge, I had designed the lampshade from a photograph so there were no dimensional specifications, rendered drawings or author advice.

There were many times in the shop where I was in over my head with this first project. Creating the components of the thin oak wood framework required numerous precision cuts with my fingers

dangerously close to the table saw blade. As a novice woodworker in trouble, many times I had to admit my unknowing and summon the shop manager to get me out of potentially dangerous situations. I completed the project shaken but unscathed. I was especially glad when I had the challenging shade assembly of the floor lamp completed.

I learned a lot about woodshop safety and Arts and Crafts design from this floor lamp project that I applied years later to other projects. It was during this floor lamp effort that I developed my procedure for cutting and assembly of the quadrilinear[3] post legs of the Morris Chair.

Cultivate Patience

Over the entire year of making the Morris Chair, there were several challenging situations that threatened the project. One was the problem with the wood itself. White Oak (Quercus alba) has always been the preferred wood of choice for Arts and Crafts furniture. My lumber dealer offered me over 50 board feet of quartersawn white oak, rare curly variety. I was happy to get this lumber. All had come from the same tree!

The intricate grain figure of the curly white oak variety was tighter and more dense than I expected. For authenticity, I wanted to build with white oak lumber and I also welcomed the rare curly grain figure for my chair. To my dismay, when I tried out some of the curly grain oak for another project, the rare curly figured wood that I bought was being destroyed in the machines I was using! This destruction started to reduce the useable wood available to complete my chair. More experienced woodworkers advised me to stop machine planing immediately and instead have this lumber machine sanded elsewhere to my specifications.

◆ ◆ ◆

For your personal safety and best project outcomes, respect the tools, materials and procedures that you will use to explore your DIY creative interests.

◆ ◆ ◆

A personally risky part of my Morris Chair effort was the mythical yet historically accurate ammonia fuming process. This dangerous procedure had to be done outside in the open air away from occupied buildings, people and pets. Modern day Arts and Crafts furniture mak-

ers no longer fume their work because of these hazards.

I wanted to fume my chair to continue to pay homage to a bygone era. Following strict precautions and rehearsal, I was able to more safely fill the fuming tent with the high levels of ammonia that atmospherically colors the wood of my Morris Chair in a more traditional way.

Other personal threats come from a workshop filled with powerful, high-speed cutting tools that require deference, patience, and respect as you enter. Your garage and your garden contain natural and man-made hazards that you'll want to manage as you are working there. Please remain awake and aware when you are taking on your new DIY adventure. Don't let your exuberance and delight with your personal discovery process prevent you from reading the fine print regarding application safety for paints or adhesives.

This precaution would apply in the kitchen as well, when rolling out a pie crust or operating an electric mixer for tasty banana nut muffins. Keep your fingers away from rotating kitchen appliances! Kitchen tools and sharp knives can pinch or cut a careless finger. On your other DIY projects in the garden involving lifting stones or wheelbarrows of soil, bend your knees as you lift. Think ahead as your gardening project might involve moving large heavy containers of growing medium. Watch your toes. And get some help for the really heavy stuff.

Please wear the recommended eye protection as you are sweat soldering your DIY copper plumbing repair. Aim your gas torch flame away from combustible floor joists. Keep your knives sharp and use them carefully as you prepare your vegetables for stir-fry.

These personal and project risks can be anticipated when you think ahead and change your action accordingly. Hearing, seeing and breathing protection is a must on every project. More simply put, take care of yourself and your exciting DIY effort.

What Did I Learn About Metamorphosis from the Morris Chair?

○ There is personal risk in creative pursuit. Your personal identity will change, both internally and externally. You will start making your own stuff. You will become a more active participant in creating the physical world that you interact with every day. You will be doing more of what you want when you take more control of your personal environment. This change in your behavior will create new relationships with your friends and family, who might be supportive of your interests. Or, they might be threatened by your personal resolve to better yourself through DIY effort.

◉ Learn to establish and accept realistic limits and boundaries for yourself. Assess your creative interests against your ability to adapt to the demands of your project. Impatience can motivate and endanger; start small and simple, then scale to larger and more complex. Seek to reduce the risk of ambition and hubris.

● Honor the limitations of the tools and materials that you use. Cultivate patience and learn the correct, safe way to operate these tools that you will use for your DIY adventure. There could be physical risk from attempting too much too soon so proceed slowly and confidently.

Now that I've heightened your interest in making your own things, let's look into the next chapter, where I will show you how by creating your stuff you can overcome fear.

CHAPTER 2:

Overcoming Fear

I was three months into the building of my Morris Chair, and I still had very little to show for my efforts other than little bundles of carefully trimmed pieces of white oak lumber. For months, I had been sawing and loosely wrapping these cryptically labeled parts of the chair in kraft paper to store them in a dusty locker. I was getting frustrated and a little fearful that I was not measuring up to some timeline I had in my mind about completion.

When you are considering your project, at any step from beginning to completion, the little voice of Fear might begin to tap you on the shoulder. Three important fears you might encounter: fear of the judgment of others, fear of the judgment of oneself, fear of choosing the wrong path.

Fear of the Judgment of Others

So far on this Morris Chair project, there had been no opportunity to glue up and complete anything. After more than 3 months of work, I had nothing assembled that I could show anyone that even looked like a chair. I could only clamp pieces together. It seemed like the other shop members had started on their projects, completed many of them, and had moved on. The Cub Scouts with their dads and the pinewood cars came and went. An elderly man, Patrick, was building a clock for each of his 5 daughters. He was racing against time and winning. Jim had been designing and building a slickly polished adaptive desk system from plywood for his home. Diane had designed and completed an entire wall system of shelves and drawers, had taken them home, and went off to get married.

There were no parts of my chair that I felt I could glue, assemble and finally complete, for fear that I would create an assembly problem later on. This reluctance was delaying my gratification. I was feeling stuck, yet I wanted to show off, get a little ego boost from other shop attendees. I wanted to know that I was on the right path. And the fears multiplied.

◆ ◆ ◆

In facing fear, recall your successful past to pave your future.

◆ ◆ ◆

As you start to consider your DIY project, remember that you've had some successes in your past that can give you the confidence to start and stay the course for your next challenge. Sometimes we start to fear when we forget our past strength. All things being equal, if you've had some success in what you have done in the past, then you can presume that your current skills, updated from what you learned before will assist you with your new challenging effort.

I had been preparing my skills for building this Morris Chair over several years of intensive focus on other smaller projects. With projects like the floor lamp, picture frame, and tabouret table, I had become familiar with the challenges of the wood, how it dulled and burned the saw blades, how it was full of internal stress that would pop out or splinter when relieved, and how the design required precision cuts and assembly.

When you recall your past success, you will have a foundation to build upon for the next challenge. Everything you know now is based on what you've learned from before. This is the origin for the confidence to test the next creative opportunity.

Back then, especially on the tabouret table, I had learned the necessity of carefully friction fitting without glue the entire assembly procedure. The interlocking nature of the joinery requires that all parts be assembled in a strict sequence. Oddly, I started risking my chair project with my impatience to have something to show for my months of effort. Don't let your impatience become an impediment to your good outcome. I learned by waiting.

Mortise and tenon joinery creates the strongest locking joints possible in woodworking. When these wood joints are locked, glued and pinned, only destructive sawing will separate the parts. And these joints are difficult to create with power tools and are time consuming to create by hand. In fact, some of the original makers in the 20th century faked their through-tenons and butt joined their designs with hidden dowels to simplify and speed the assembly just to make

the finished piece look authentic. Close scrutiny by a trained eye will detect the deception.

And my past experience in assembly of the tabouret table showed me, on a smaller scale, the importance of dry fitting all the way through in antic-

ipation of the final assembly. In a toss to authenticity, I had customized and complicated the published plan by bringing the four legs of the table up through the tabletop. This meant that the entire leg assembly had to be complete at glue up before I could align the circular top onto the pyramid-topped legs. Everything had to be built square from the very first leg support months before. Eventually that glue up and assembly became a memorable Gordian knot nightmare of my own doing, as I had to sequence, assemble and clamp all parts of the table before the time and temperature dependent glue began to cure and set. I thought I had learned this lesson from the table applicable to the chair. But I forgot.

In the following months, somehow I had forgotten the successful projects of my past. With the forgetting I started to question myself about the best time to start assembly. I was being impatient. I had forgotten how well it all turned out when I resisted the need to pro-

duce something to show someone else. I had forgotten how the success with the tabouret table was a lesson in waiting, careful planning and then execution when the time was right.

When you are working on your emerging creative project, don't let the others around you threaten your successful outcome with their real or imagined expectations of your effort.

Fear of Judgment From Oneself

Take it easy on yourself. Maybe the top reason that you've not been making your own things to this point is because you have self-limiting beliefs about yourself and your abilities. You might have a standard in your mind about your outcome that is holding you back, based on someone else's evaluation of your creative skills many years before. As a result you might be thinking: "Whatever I try is going to turn out wrong."

Be cautious about your self-evaluation based on some one else's opinion in the past. I'd like to remind you that that was then and this is now. And I hope that you've learned a lot and grown a lot since then. Besides, you don't need to show anyone your projects until you want to. What about giving it one more try to the effort and then see where you are?

Admittedly, it can take a lot of time, energy and work to make your own things. It can be downright hard sometimes to face the facts about what you might find out about yourself. You might be reminded that you really aren't the next Picasso, Rembrandt or Norm Abrams, the well-respected woodcrafter on the PBS TV network, or that you aren't the next on-line cooking diva, knitting hot shot or home repair fix-it man. What about approaching your creative effort without comparison and self-judgment? Dare I say, for the fun and challenge of it?

Our self-judgments of creative abilities might be overly harsh and self-critical when we question our work or our ability to take on and complete a new task.

It's also tricky to safely calibrate our skills where we might have more hubris and pluck than is safe or recommended. You might be wildly successful even as a successful outcome is not guaranteed. How would you define your successful outcome anyway? Avoid having your outcome dictate your self-worth and esteem.

◆ ◆ ◆

Generally, you are your own worst critic.

◆ ◆ ◆

So to take yourself to task over a judgment you've made about your project is hugely detrimental to you. As long as you are applying yourself with your best effort, that is all that can be hoped for. After all, you are the one who will have to live with it, be it the drywall mud that you've applied to patch your wall, or the biscotti dough that you've just stirred up to bake those crispy slices that you made yourself! What you do will be your best result...until next time. Until then, who knows?

When I decided to start my Morris Chair, I had some big expectations. I knew that I was going to build the piece as authentically as possible. I wanted the chair to reflect the spirit of a Gustav Stickley-designed Drop Arm Spindle Side Morris

Chair. I knew that I wanted to add subtle design accents like the ebony dot inlay in the thru-arm tenons that would subtly make the chair distinctively my own.

You might find that these self-critical evaluations of your outcomes can pop up at anytime in the process, not only at completion. Much like an airplane in flight requires constant course correction to bring it to a safe landing, there are course corrections and technique changes during the creative process where destructive self-judgment can creep in. Strike a measured balance between the execution of your project and the critical self-evaluation that is bound to happen. It's going to be good whatever way it turns out! You are doing something creative for yourself.

You can celebrate the ways that you are succeeding in your effort and look to the way that you are feeling self-reliant and accomplished. Plan all your creative efforts to be non-critical, low-stress events where the risk is not too high if you run across "some bumps in the road." You can celebrate the incremental surprises and successes as you move toward your feelings of accomplishment.

If you've decided to make pancakes on a range top griddle on a Saturday morning, and you overcook and burn a few, you can recover quickly by moving those off to the side and starting over with a new attempt. It'll be no big deal! Enjoy the good ones and learn from the others. You'll want your first projects to be easy and fun learning experiences where you are able to enjoy the "ride" along the journey. As you acquire more success and more self-confidence you'll build self-reliance more quickly with a series of repeatable good outcomes.

Fear of the Wrong Path

Admittedly, it is difficult to always know if you are moving along the best way when you are mid-project. If you are starting out on your creative adventure on projects where you've not got much experience or knowledge, the self-doubt along the way can become crippling. It is at these points where it is a good idea to check in, if you can, with someone who has useful advice for you.

But your advisors might not know the best way for you. Please don't totally surrender your common sense when you encounter a mentor or advisor who appears to have more knowledge or experience than you. Take a measured approach and gather your information from more than one source if you are unsure. Blindly following instructions without question might put you where *they* think that you want to be instead of where *you* want to be. Keep your mind about you and keep your focus on your project and your best outcome.

For the construction of the chair, I consulted four different published plan books, none of which were complete. All of them contained measurement and math errors and omissions. One lacked critical measurements and completely omitted any ideas for the bottom cushion support. One plan book deceptively showed a photo of a spindle side Morris Chair on the cover, but the inside plans were for a slat side Morris Chair. One plan offering appeared to be the most detailed, but the angles of joinery were achievable only with computer assisted (CAD) cutting and routing machines. Using a computer to control the cutting tools were not part of my Morris Chair vision. None of the plan descriptions contained reliable information about authentic finishing techniques. Metaphorically, I was working without a net from the start.

Nevertheless, I was curious to learn if I had the skills to take on the iconic Arts and Crafts Morris Chair. I had not done this sized project before and I knew no one who had. I took the best parts of each of the plans, and prepared to start. In previous years before starting my Morris Chair project, I had carefully examined original Morris Chairs for construction details when I found them in museums and antique showrooms. And I had had a few years of practice on other completed Arts and Crafts Movement projects, so I felt like I was qualified to start. But did I really "know?"

◆ ◆ ◆

Follow your curiosity, assess your skills, and begin your effort without judgment.

◆ ◆ ◆

I felt like I was very much out there on my own with this effort. You might have that same thought as you entertain thoughts of awakening your latent creativity. From the start, please recognize that I congratulate you for your bravery to seek out and commit to your own starter project. I realize that it can be more than a little scary stepping off your known path to choose a fork in the road that hopefully will lead to new personal insights rooted in self-expression and self-evaluation. Please be gentle with yourself as you explore.

If you have lived in Westernized society for any period of time, and you start along this path of creative exploration I offer just a word of caution. You are going to make a judgment of the quality and value of your creative work just as you have in previous efforts. Trust me on this. In your own way you will self evaluate your efforts on a scale between the two extremes of Good and Bad. *This. Will. Happen.* I encourage you to adopt a softer gaze, to see your work simply as it occurs. Please do not see your creative output as a measure of your self-worth. Your creative outcome on this must not become a measure of anything. But you will judge, you will evaluate and you will compare.

Especially at your first effort, the self-recrimination and self-questioning will start. As a novice, just out of the gate, this will be the time when you will personally set your "bar" about your abilities and success with this effort to the future. You've already graded your efforts for so many other parts of your life. For example, you might recall that you label yourself as a good or bad automobile driver. If asked, you might say that you lack the green thumb required for success with plants. All these self-evaluations and self-beliefs result from assessments of yourself; from yourself or the appraisal from others.

Observe caution with your ego at this point of your new path, especially for your first efforts. Please see the journey as creative and whatever outcome as only an outcome. Reduce the tendency to attach any significance to the initial outcomes. If you find yourself discouraged, this could be a learning point for you. What could you do next time for a different outcome? If you surprised yourself with outcomes that exceeded your expectations, what can you learn from this experience to support you to have a similar outcome or better the next time? These outcomes, of any ranking or value, can be celebrated merely because you completed it!

Please realize that the preparation for my Morris Chair started decades earlier, perhaps with a careful introduction to various powerful tools led by a forgotten teacher. At that time, I might have developed respect for the cutting and shaping power in the shop by successfully sawing one piece of wood. I still fear the cutting power of these tools. I was quite fearful of sudden loud noises as a child, so I imagine that even for me to flip the switch to start the motor would have been an important step for me on the way to making my own things. Start where you are and advance as you can.

I encourage you to celebrate the beginning steps of any mental or physical effort that will guide you on the path to your creative interest. If you've never cooked for yourself and you have an audacious thought for cooking at home for a dinner party at a later time, start with boiling the water in a pan on the range top. Did you achieve repeatable success? Then move to the next step. Plan the next dinner party after you've spent some time in the kitchen with a series of repeatable successes.

What Have I Learned About Fear
from the Morris Chair?

○ Others are going to judge you. It can be scary to start your creative effort or to start doing for yourself in new areas of your life. When you choose to take on a creative project, especially for your first effort, others around you are going to make an evaluation of your outcome. As you did to reduce risk in Chapter 1, you will want to start small and work larger to reduce fear as you have more success and affirming outcomes. There is no reason why you need to show your early efforts if by your evaluation there is more learning and work for you to do. This is your effort, not anyone else's.

○ It's going to happen that you are going to judge yourself on your efforts. You are going to compare your efforts with others. That behavior is an unwelcomed result of 21st century living in the Western world. You must not allow your early outcomes on tough projects to determine your self-worth and value. Your sense of personal resourcefulness and self-determination will grow as you apply your learning to future projects.

● All along the process, it's possible that questions will arise about whether you are doing this correctly. Often, there is no one to ask to affirm your path. You might question your choices for the next step. Even if there is a source of respected knowledge, resist the thought to totally trust that information. Make your best guess based on the information that you have at the time, and remain flexible and aware of your options. Don't be too harsh with demands for a particular outcome as you take in lessons along the way.

Now that I've shown you ways to manage fear in your creative efforts, let's look at Chapter 3 – Letting Go.

CHAPTER 3:

Letting Go

You might be wondering when does the fun part start? With all this risk and fear is it dangerous for you to try out this new adventure of being more self-sufficient and humanly creative? Where is the safety, relaxation and ease you might expect from making with your hands for yourself?

Let me assure you the anticipated benefits are within the activity! Generally, you'll find that once you've chosen your project, your path, and set your resolve, the road will widen and open to you. This expansive opening happened for me, mid-project, shortly after I relaxed my churning mind about what I thought I "ought" to be completing and instead re-committed myself to the Morris Chair project for as long as it would take. I had become the impatient, rigid, ambitious one who was making this effort harder than it needed to be.

See What Happens

Forget your self-perpetuated rules, and demands of guaranteed success, to see what happens.

In the first three months of the Morris Chair experience, somehow I had been feeling pressure to have something to show myself and others. After I relaxed my internal tension about keeping a rigid production schedule, I found that my expectations of the projected outcome had been blocking the satisfaction I'd been seeking along the way. It was better to relax and enjoy the ride. What I was doing to tackle the Morris Chair project was hard enough. I was making the project more difficult than it needed to be. I found benefit by striking a balance between rigor and relax.

◆ ◆ ◆

Advice and plans are only a guide for your creative expression.

◆ ◆ ◆

No one explores their creative potential thinking that they are going to purposely do a mediocre job. Everyone wants to, at minimum satisfy his or her inner critic. If you link your outcome on first time projects to your self-worth, you are setting yourself up for potential frustration and disappointment. So you've got to get some distance from your early expectations and relax on this. And make a pact with yourself to do as best you can with what you know and what you've learned.

When you first start out, I hope that you are going to do pretty well. If you are learning to sew on a button, you're probably getting the hang of it after a few false  starts. You are taking small steps and learning as you go. After you've gotten more practice in handling the needle and thread, your quality will improve as your learning curve flattens. Then the routine starts to take over, as creative solutions aren't needed. What was initially excitement with the formerly new skill starts to become routine. Congratulations!

What was exciting about feeding lumber into a saw the first time quickly became routine after numerous passes. This happened for me with cutting 30 spindles for the Morris Chair. I had already figured out the procedure that then became routine for multiple passes across the whistling blade.

What might have been thrilling for you as your own sous chef trimming vegetables for your first pasta primavera become routine and no longer challenging after you've done that task a few times.

When I was caning the Morris Chair seat cushion support, the repetitive weaving of the strands was mind numbing, and the potential for error was very high. More than a few times, I had to back up and remove strands. It took longer to cane the seat than I had expected. I had to dial back my expectation that I was going to be perfect on my first caning project. I did okay, but even now there remain some weaving errors that do not pass close inspection. I didn't see those subtle missteps until I had completed the entire weaving. Repetition leads to routine. Routine leads to dimmed awareness, then to mistakes. Perfection becomes the enemy of good.

In those situations of repetitive activity, it is hard to remain alert to potential errors because of the routine. My antidote for the expert's

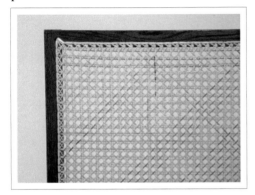

fatigue is to try to adopt the beginner's mind of Zen Buddhism and to refer back to the early lessons gained during first attempts. Going back to the fundamentals is a good practice to adopt in any creative pursuit.

It was only after I relaxed my expectations of perfect outcomes that I realized that I was starting to enjoy the creative journey again. I decided that it was okay to be the Chair Guy in the shop instead of the guy that took too much time on the table saw. With my acceptance of that change of mind, it seemed like some of the shop members became interested in my project. I felt supported and a part of the shop team instead of the solitary outsider toiling on his masterpiece. It seemed different now, like they wanted me to succeed.

Over time, some shop members became curious about Arts and Crafts period ideals and started their own little projects. I was eager to help out, to advise. Some began building mirror frames in white oak. I enjoyed being the person they would ask about design or finishing techniques. I was having early success with my reformed mindset and relaxed attitude that I hoped would continue. I decided to focus on authenticity and craftsmanship of my project, instead of my imagined timelines or the comparisons I had of others. This chair effort was going to take as long as it took. And that was going to be okay.

You might find that your relaxation into your new identity as a maker, a builder, a creator will attract the interest of others who don't

currently make their own stuff. At first, they might question your motivations for this interest. When you are painting your own walls or rehabbing your own bathroom, your friends will certainly notice. It might bother them as it bothered you, when they realize that their work-a-day world experience is missing a creative human element. Instead of stepping robotically through their workweek, they could be accessing new and wonderful aspects of their creative humanity.

What could be the lifestyle benefit and latent value of your daily experience when you knead your bread dough into the daily bread that feeds you? This is more than a metaphorical construct. Could making by hand be a key to the elusive work/life balance? How would your friendships transform if you fed, clothed and delighted them with the efforts of your hands?

I predict there will be a cascading effect of creativity and personal satisfaction for you when you let yourself start to explore more of your life through making something in your world with your hands. As your skills and confidence increase, you can control more of what is happening around you. Your sense of resilience and self-reliance will increase over time. Building on each effort, you might discover that you can advance from sewing on buttons to knitting, repainting your wall, or repairing your fence. And the expansion of skills and self-empowerment is going to feel great!

You Are Not Alone, So Don't Remain Aloof

Anytime when you are planning or working on learning your craft, it can be tempting to imagine that you toil alone. You might imagine that no one else is doing what you are doing. You might even get a little smug about that, mistakenly believing that you have found the true path. You might dangerously conclude that the others are lost or unknowing. And that would be your illusion.

Admittedly, there were times in the shop when I believed that I was the real woodworker and that I would find my answers from within. After all, I was working in solid furniture grade lumber, building by hand in iconic designs, while others outside the shop chose to buy objects made from plywood, wood scraps and resin, made in multiples by machines. After all, I was building for myself what others viewed only in opulent homes and enlightened art museums. More to the point, there was a philosophical and historical underpinning to my craft!

◆ ◆ ◆

Use the knowledge you have and ask for the knowledge you have not. Then step forward.

◆ ◆ ◆

I wanted this to be my chair, one tree, one craftsman, built with my hands and my knowledge. But there were questions I could not answer as I went deeper into my project. The plan books I consulted did not address the steam-bending of the back slats. No one I knew had built his or her own chair, at least not a Morris Chair. The apocryphal mystery of atmospheric fuming with ammonia to chemically darken the wood, outdoors in a tent, remained unsolved and possibly deadly. Do I raise the wood grain with water if I fume? Is grain alcohol the best solvent for shellac? Is pore filling of the wood figure a good idea? What about using solvents like amyl acetate as a finish dryer? Where to find traditional upholsterers capable of putting Marshall coil springs in pockets sewn inside seat cushions? Do I build the chair square for all joinery and then shorten the back legs to make the chair sit back ? By how much?

The answers were shrouded in mystery somewhere between myth and mainstream. The truth remained elusive.

Sometimes, as you explore further into your newly found creative interests, you might get slowed by unknowns. What about latex trim paint over oil? Bread flour or all-purpose flour? L or M grade copper pipe for plumbing repair? Knit with wool or acrylic? Propane or

MAPP gas for sweat soldering? Gate or ball water valves? Do I seal the water stains on the wall with lacquer and then paint? Do I leave lead-based paint or remove it? What is a vapor barrier for wall insulation, and where does it go?

Some answers are known by the people who already do what you want to do. Sometimes the answers are not where you'd expect. Other answers will be yours to find through trial and error. The bakers in the artisanal bakery know the flour they like to use. Knitters might select yarn by feel. Plumbers can advise on the grade of copper water pipe for different applications. Painters know how they seal water stains in walls once the leak has been fixed. Gate or ball valves; either will work. The experience of others is a teacher for you.

I wanted to build my chair with steam bent slats. Design authenticity required it. I had questions about getting the right materials. Would I use kiln dried (6% moisture) or green (12% moisture) lumber? Most lumber mills routinely kiln dry their commercial furniture grade lumber before sale which I began to "hear" from experienced woodworkers was not acceptable for bending. When I told my wood supplier of my interest in steam bending he advised that I buy from his reserve of quarter-sawn green oak and try bending that. But he knew nothing about thickness and bend radius by species because he had never steam bent wood. I built bending forms based on guesswork and guidance I found from an on-line tool supplier who had a technical chart of wood bending information by species. I was able to heat and bend the oak slats by trial and error in the steam filled sap vats at my parents' maple syrup farm during the off-season. Again, this was try and fail until it worked.

When you are focused on your creative project, the answers will arrive as you begin to rub shoulders with people who share your passion. Always use your best judgment regardless of the source of information.

The Morris Chair is an adjustable recliner. The back cushion support pivots on

pegs and is held by pegs. The chair geometry is critical for comfort. I learned later that some have said that a chair is the most difficult piece of furniture to design and build. I don't know if that is true, but I wanted to be sure that I was creating my chair for a comfortable sitting experience. Over the months, I actively sought and carefully compared the recline angle of antique and reproduction Morris Chairs. I found that the backward tilt geometry of the base assembly was different for every chair. I continued to build, and soon the chair was complete except for the tilt, fuming and finish. A cut awry, too much or too meager, would destroy a year of effort.

My answer for this important problem could not come from within myself. I tapped the zeitgeist and my pilgrimage led me to travel over 400 miles North to Manlius, NY, to a small, well-equipped woodshop in the L. & J.G. Stickley Furniture factory where these chairs are made now as they were then, a century before. I had come to solicit the L. & J.G. Stickley custom shop woodworkers on their lunch break for a prescriptive reading. Undeterred, that afternoon I asked the Oracle I found in the back shop at L. & J.G. Stickley one question and it answered.

Perfect is the Enemy of the Good

As you become more fluent in your creative expression, you will start to question what perfection means to you. If you've taken up knitting on needles as a way to connect your daily life to your humanity, you will be constantly comparing each new stitch in relationship to the completed ones.

◆ ◆ ◆

Aim for perfection; settle for the best.

◆ ◆ ◆

Your objective as an early knitter might be individual symmetrical stitches that, when viewed in the aggregate, blend in easily with the others to form a wider expanse of uniformity. But this is handwork, so there will be subtle variation along the journey. When you step back and view the entirety of your project, if it's drywall repair or mending your rustic stonewall, these small faults diminish over the wider area. You would get nowhere on your project if you stopped and re-knit every slight variation that signaled a challenge to your personal notion of perfection. Correct the big stuff, live with the small stuff. Forgive the low-grade offenses, notice and fix the greater insult. Live and learn from the flaws that remain.

There are imperfections buried in my Morris Chair. In my opinion, there aren't many, but I know where they are and I'm irked when I see them. Then I remember. A story resides in the imperfection. In those errors lie the lessons for me.

Some occurred because of lapses in my judgment at the time. When I see them I'm reminded to be more vigilant to the future.

Some errors remain visible in the chair because I lost my awareness. I am reminded that awareness is fleeting.

Some errors occurred because I was confused. I am reminded of my impatience and limitations.

These errors are what I recall, my personal assessment of what I see. No one reports them as I see them, and no one cares as much as I do. Besides, they blend into the whole so much as to become insignificant. With so much correct in the design, who cares about "the small stuff?" Despite all these personal challenges to perfection, and my harsh personal assessment of myself, in September 2010 I was asked to demonstrate my Morris Chair at the Smithsonian Institution to a group of Master level decorative art students from the Corcoran School of Art.

Als Ik Kan

to the best of my ability
(from the Flemish)

The motto of the highly influential Gustav Stickley to describe his work.

What Have I Learned About Letting Go from the Morris Chair?

○ To expect impatience with yourself and your skills. Expect to come to your creative project with all kinds of perceived notions and self-perpetuated rules about how you will do on your effort. Upon reflection, your self-assessment might require a change. Guidance from yourself and from others must be assessed in the light of your experience. You learn that it's best to adopt a beginner's mind, so that you can be open to what happens. Your personal identity and beliefs about yourself will change as you take on the mantle of creative human, *Homo sapiens faber.* Others will see you differently. Others might change because of your interest in making with your hands.

◉ You might think that you know from within. Your personal knowledge goes only so far. Assess your role in the collective creative experience. You do not toil alone. Ask for the knowledge of others more experienced than you. Beware of thoughts of self-importance and entitlement. Others have information and insight for you.

● Creative pursuit will tempt you with ideals of perfection. Perfection is an aim, not the goal. There is story in the imperfection. You will make mistakes and you will evaluate yourself. Creative exploration has a learning curve that results in errors, requires rejection of some errors, and an acceptance of some errors. A lapse in judgment calls for more vigilance next time. A loss of awareness reminds that awareness is a vagabond wanderer. Confusion signals a change in your perspective that points to your limits.

Now that I've shown you the learning that might be available to you from letting go within your creative efforts, let's look at Chapter 4: Best Choice, Bad Choices.

◆ ◆ ◆

CHAPTER 4:

Best Choice, Bad Choices

Your attempts to explore your creative experience will involve choices. Breaking this down into smaller pieces, more specifically, as you move through your challenging project you will be making choices that will either advance or delay your effort. You will make good choices that will confirm and advance your effort. And you will make bad choices that will delay but not deter you from completing your creative project.

For example, for your container garden, a good choice would be to buy and plant new seeds in the gardening season rather than to plant the seeds in your drawer from a year ago because you procrastinated. Either way, either choice, there will be an outcome. You can plant what you want, but more plants will grow from fresh seed than old seed.

For painting a wide expanse of a hallway wall, a paint roller would generally be the better choice instead of the paintbrush that you would use to cut in the trim. For your first time of painting a wall, if you chose the paint brush to paint the wall you would quickly learn from that experience that the paint roller would do a better job, more quickly, for the next time. You will learn to choose the right tool for the job.

Not to belabor the point, but some bad choices are inconsequential, while others can have seriously bad outcomes. For example, selecting a fine grit of 120 sandpaper where a coarse, deeper cutting 80 grit abrasive is required, will probably not doom your first timer project. But you are not going to achieve your desired outcome either with this choice. Later on, you might look back with a smile at lessons learned as you wonder about that choice. Forgive yourself, you were just learning. But the consequences are not always benign.

When I was learning other life lessons on the tabouret table project, I unwittingly made a bad decision and chose to use a handheld router to trim the circular edge of the tabletop. Oops! In an instant I learned I had made a hopelessly wrong choice! In review after that incident, where the power router bit snagged and carved too deeply into the edge of the tabletop, I learned that I should have used a slower, more deliberate method. In this case I had to scrap that carefully selected tabletop, with the time and lumber in it, and start again. This was a setback in my project timeline, but I also learned valuable lessons.

Forgiving Yourself

Daily living involves learning from good and bad choices. Forgive yourself.

Despite all these cautions, you will bravely move forward in your effort, make your bad choice, recover and move on after learning. You will re-paint, re-cut, re-think and recover. I had admired the Morris Chair for years, but the precision and knowledge required to complete the chair project was more than I could take on as a beginner. Early on I made a lot of bad choices that slowed my advance before I made better choices where I could step forward with confidence.

I chewed up a lot of wood on the table saw making the little thin parts of the framework for the lampshade. Lots of trial and error.

Lots of forward steps and a few stops, retreats and renewed starts along the way. That's the nature of experimentation. Early efforts created the hard won learning steps built toward more woodworking mastery for the Morris Chair.

◆ ◆ ◆

Recover, re-commit and re-start after a bad choice.

◆ ◆ ◆

When you're working on your creative project, you will learn about resilience. You will test your resilience after you've made a choice that sets you back and you have to re-group. Several times, I've had to recover from mistakes that I made on very visible joinery. I hate that moment when I'm focused on doing my best on a critical procedure...and I blow it. This doesn't happen often but when it does it ain't pretty.

It's like the bottom just dropped out of my soul and I am in free-fall down a dark mineshaft. My breathing stops, and I stare at the error with my mind racing: first with disbelief and denial, second with self-loathing, and third with scrambled thoughts of possible exits from this self-inflicted visual wound.

In this case, well over six months into the project, I was working on the arm of my Morris Chair, I knew this would be a critical cut. I planned it out on paper and rehearsed the cuts with the tools. But...I unwittingly made a drastic error in measurement and boldly cut the

mortise through the arm, off center, in the wrong place!

Immediately I felt faint, weak in the knees and the droning of saws and the workshop clatter slowed to silence. My creative spirit left me, and my Morris Chair project turned to scrap before my eyes. In the past, I had made errors with power tools on the room screen, but recovered nicely and finished the piece with hand chisels to cut the bowties. Other errors at other times I had turned into design opportunities. But this egregious blunder was out there for me and everyone to see, every time anyone sat in the chair.

You will feel emotionally tested if your actions or the actions of others cause your creative effort to be derailed like this. But you cannot bottom out and quit. Life goes on, and so did my project, and so will yours.

Why did this happen? Was it loss of awareness? Do I blame a lapse in my 3-D spatial aptitude? What was I _not_ thinking? To recover, I had to forgive myself. I had to come to terms with my project and the flaw that I caused. I had worked so hard to approach perfection, and now this self inflicted torment. I had to stop and re-adjust my expectations.

To regroup I recalled once again that I would build this chair. Over recent months, this chair had become an aspect of my personal identity. It had started to consume much of my energy. It was all that I talked about in polite conversation.

Now that there was a glaring mistake that I couldn't gloss over or finesse, I had to decide what to do. I knew that I would continue. I knew that I would press forward. But I didn't want this mistake that I un-intentionally caused. I could not scrap the arm; I had no extra material. I could not design my way out of this.

I did the best I could do by finding a section of wavy figured curly quartersawn face grain and I plugged the hole. Now I live with the memories.

There. You can see it. It's along the side of the through

tenon of the front leg. The plug does not exactly match the surrounding wood and now, years later, I don't notice it all that much. It's a flaw that's become part of the story, much like the desirable and naturally occurring slubs and flaws that occur in linen fabric or full grain cowhide. The creases and scars in leather and fabric are expected, exposed and excused. Can I forgive myself for my measurement error as it became a lesson learned? Does the importance of the transgression fade with time? There is no going back; the flaw is now a part of the chair. A story resides in the imperfection.

Mistakes

What I thought was all wrong. Mistakes become legend. There is always something you can do, always something that you can learn.

When you decide to start making more of the things in your life, perhaps planting, learning a musical instrument, or making your favorite dessert pie, you will hold certain thoughts in your mind about how you should think about these things. Maybe you believe that you must have a large plot of land to plant, but later learn that there are many people who plant, grow and give away their extra vegetables from small containers on their condo balcony. Maybe you think that learning to play the piano is too difficult to enjoy, when the reality is that there are only 12 notes that repeat to combine in complex patterns. Maybe you question your ability to bake your favorite pie because of the filling or the pastry crust, when in reality there are so many options and solutions to choose from.

◆ ◆ ◆

As you explore more of your creative
expression, expect to continue to be surprised.

◆ ◆ ◆

I had seen, studied and built American Arts and Crafts Movement furniture for several years. In 1999, I was on the cusp of a revelation. I was soon to be shown that what I thought I knew was wrong.

Because of my direct experience to this point, I believed that major period makers like Gustav Stickley, his brothers and others made their furniture from American quartersawn white oak with very crisp 90 degree joinery. The very definition of A and C furniture was (1) built of white oak, and (2) rectilinear in form (straight lines with square corners). I was building my chair to these rigid specifications of species and square-ness to insure that my project would truly be authentic and correct. Or so I thought.

You might be surprised at the wide variety of options available to you for expressing your desire to explore your creative humanity. For example, if you were to take an interest in singing, what you learn about singing might challenge or even threaten what you thought you knew.

The cage doors of my creative expectations were about to get rattled during the year of the Chair. For many years before the start of the Morris Chair, I had taken an annual pilgrimage to the Grove Park Inn in Asheville, N.C., for the Arts and Crafts Conference, headed up by Bruce Johnson. It is a weekend conference of devotees, where they sit in these chairs and talk reverentially about the square brown furniture of white oak. During the years of researching and building my Morris Chair, I traveled to other important Arts and Crafts Movement destinations for ideas. One of my stops was the Stickley Factory in Manlius, NY, where they still to this day build brown oak furniture in rectilinear form. Another stop on my Morris Chair walkabout was

the epicenter of the A & C Movement; Craftsman Farms in Morris Plains, NJ that Gus Stickley built and where he lived.

Sited on the Farms property, the clubhouse where the Stickley family lived is a sort of holy site for me. It is a secular Mecca for the Arts & Crafts Movement zealot. When Tommy McPherson, the director of the museum showed me around the place, I saw the original, iconic, one-of-a-kind square oak museum quality pieces built for the clubhouse that the adherents speak of in hushed tones. This was a heady experience for me to be there among those relics. But at the top of the stairs in the Girl's Room, two of the basic tenets of my Arts and Crafts Movement belief were about to be shattered.

As I entered the room, Tommy explained,"The drawer pulls of the Gustav Stickley designed originals in the room are highlighted in shades of blue and silver. The closet door is trimmed in gumwood."

I looked more carefully about the room. Gumwood? I noticed that the closet door and trimwork were indeed not oak, and had been cut at an oblique angle, slanting dramatically upward, decidedly not even close to a 90-degree angle! What I saw as mistakes were not mistakes. This had been Gustav Stickley's home. This is the way Stickley wanted it when he lived there!

Shocked, I whispered, "What about an oak door, trimmed in oak at 90 degree angles?" Tommy went on to explain that Stickley and others experimented with other species of wood and other colors from nature that complemented the brown tones of the fumed oak. The rhomboid closet door resulted shortly after construction in 1911, when the foundation settled and the door began to stick in the doorframe. So they cut the door to make it fit where it currently hangs.

Hmmm...not oak and not square. And blue and silver accents?

Before this epiphany, what I had thought about Arts & Crafts Movement design motifs wasn't really wrong; it's just that my concept of materials and methods were too limited; too narrow. Evidently there was more to this enduring Movement than I knew, more than dark oak and square angles. I had been shown a new way to view my work, to view myself and my beliefs. The palette of acceptable expression had just been enlarged.

I came away from the Farms with a changed mind. What I thought was rigid was flexible. What I viewed as mistakes was enshrined as legend. What I believed to be true became a larger truth. I had gone to my Mecca and had been changed by what I saw there.

You might be challenged by what you learn about yourself when you take on your creative endeavor. You might begin to see your mistakes and the creative errors of others on the journey as launching points for new ways of expression. I hope that you can explore beyond what you thought you knew, to change your preconceived beliefs about the basis for your creative interests.

Stop, Consider, Retreat

Success on your project will be punctuated with stops and starts. It is not possible to smoothly transition from action to action, unless you've been down that road of discovery before through rehearsal or previous experience. The good choice that you make will speed you quickly to your next decision point. The bad choices that you make should cause you some pause to consider the next step. That's what you should do. Stop and evaluate. Consider. Forward action on your project is not always measured by unfocused movement for the sake of movement.

◆ ◆ ◆

Repeat the best choices. Recover from the poor choices. Retreat, re-focus, and resume.

◆ ◆ ◆

Recreating an authentic Arts and Crafts finish that looks old on new wood is steeped in myth and mystery. The exact formulas often vanished with the death of furniture companies and the men who ran them. Historically, some of the materials used were poisonous, corrosive or quickly hazardous to the woodcrafter's health. The color palette of Arts & Crafts furniture finishes vary greatly, centering around shades of brown, orange, red and black and are difficult to recreate with original methods.

Original finishes on original antiques have oxidized to a mellow patina for 100+ years. Creating a contemporary yet authentic finish using safer components requires lots of repetitive color matching, testing and comparison.

Shellac, in various shades, and various dilutions compliments and enhances the overall look. All of these elixirs take time to make, test and apply.

Your effort in creative discovery for yourself might remind you of the tabletop toy that grinds to the edge of a table, senses the edge, backs away and only to pick a new path for travel in another direction. Your creative effort allows for changes in intention and direction.

It's okay to make mistakes. Allow for it. Learning is dependent on missteps. Assume that it will take longer to do, that you will not have enough material, that you will not have the exact tool -- you will have to improvise. You are going to have to think to advance. Sometimes think quickly for best choices, as in fractions of seconds -- as when sawing and gluing, baking or photography. Sometimes you are going to have to ponder many choices and select one path -- as in home repair or garden plot preparation.

Lessons Learned from Best Choice, Bad Choices

○ There will be advances and retreats. Bad choices will test your resilience. You might surprise yourself when you learn of your capacity for resilience. You will recover from bad choices, even drastic project threatening errors. Errors could be time-consuming and benign, or very quick and appear to be devastating. Vice versa. You will question your resolve to complete. You might feel like giving up. Bad choices can be a springboard for new approaches to advance to good choices.

◉ Don't be daunted by decision-making. When you commit to a creative journey to reclaim more of your humanity, remain aware and prepare to be surprised by what you can learn. Narrowness of approach leads to narrow outcomes. Be open to new ideas even when you think you know everything. Maintain focus on a future end result but prepare to change your approach as you make both your best choices and your bad choices.

● All creative journey movement is not constant and is not always forward toward your end result. It's okay to retreat. Then recover, refocus and resume. All decisions for your effort will not be known at the start. You might not know, in review, why you chose to pick a certain path. There is rarely enough time, material, physical space, mental energy, guidance from others or support for this effort when you are truly testing your choice to explore more of your human creative potential.

Now that I've shown you the importance of best choices and resilience, let's move on to Chapter 5: Belief.

CHAPTER 5:

Belief

We've looked at how change, fear, acceptance and choice will affect your interest in creative exploration. But the large part of approaching your creative endeavor is...belief. Your personal belief in yourself. Your personal belief in your ability to take on a creative effort. Your ability to see your effort as a worthy goal. You've got to believe that you can do what you've decided do. If you don't think that you can do it, you won't. But even then, I'd encourage you to give it a chance. In this chapter, you'll learn to honor your belief in yourself, honor your belief in the concept/project, and honor your belief in the outcome.

Honor Your Belief in Yourself

Wear the mantle of a courageous, creative person as you approach your work. There will be times when you will question your worthiness to even consider this creative effort. Those feelings will emerge as they have for craftspeople and self-sufficient people for millennia. For example, if you are interested in reducing your dependence on pre-packaged convenience food and you begin to cook and bake for yourself, you will advance in your skills with practice -- but occasionally you might burn or over-season something that you are preparing. It's un-

derstandable to doubt your cooking when you've created something that even you are unwilling to eat.

◆ ◆ ◆

This is your choice to do as you want, to feel accomplished in what you do, to see your creative exploration as another avenue to knowing yourself.

◆ ◆ ◆

When I was planning for my Morris Chair, I was surprised by how traditional I became in my approach to the effort. When you make your own stuff, you'll find that some aspects of your personality will inform the work.

In the earlier projects like the picture frame, floor lamp and tabouret table, I had experimented with modern water-based and alcohol-based aniline dyes and wipe-on varnishes. Modern finishing techniques produce exciting approximations of 100 year old oxidized surface patinas, but in this instance for the chair I was chasing a different outcome. Instead, I knew that authenticity required that I fume the chair with dangerous ammonia fumes, and mix the shellac from flakes in a solvent as was done a century before. For my Morris Chair, I rejected all modernity with the challenge of replicating the craft as it was a hundred years before.

As I planned for the chair, the revered Arts and Crafts ideals of head, heart and hands emerged to influence the process as it did for makers more than a century before. The beguiling visual simplicity masked the complexity of construction. During my project I felt as though I was in league with crafters from the past who struggled against similar issues that had dogged them and vexed me during my building phase.

I wanted steam bent slats in my chair even when some plan books suggested cutting the arched pieces from kiln dried lumber using a bandsaw to cut the curve.

I didn't want foam rubber in my seat cushions. Even the best foam rubber degrades into crumbles in a few decades so I chose internal coil springs for authenticity. I intended that this chair would outlive me and become a treasured heirloom bequeathed to a younger family member or close friend. I wanted every through tenon and its mortise to be genuine, even as a shopmate told me that I was taking too long with the chair. He said that he'd have just made up the fake end of the tenon and glued it to the legs. He said that nobody would know. But I would know. This was my belief, my chair, and I would always know the way that I made it.

As your creative skills become more consistent, you might decide to invite a group of friends to dinner at your place. I would find it surprising if you weren't a little anxious about your self-judgments, the possible judgments of your friends. It's not easy producing a dining experience on time and on demand. I know that when I've planned for that sort of social food event my time in the kitchen can get tense. But you don't have to ever cook for anyone else. Start small and easily managed and then expand if you want.

When you are working on your creative project, you might find that you invest yourself completely in the work and that time just seems to fly by when you are on task. Often, with your newfound passion, the challenge will be to judiciously integrate your new interest into a life already filled with important obligations.

In my case, the public shop where I worked on the Morris Chair was limited to six hours

total per week, and I was sharing workspace with five to eight other hobbyists. I disliked those limits but those limits also allowed me to consider and plan my next steps without hurry. During the time away from the shop, I could consider my next steps and plan to steward my time wisely.

Even more vulnerably, you might sometimes feel like you don't deserve to be successful with your effort. This mindset can be a hidden reason why people don't start with their own independent creative endeavor. You might feel that you need to give yourself permission or to allow yourself to awaken your maker self. You might question yourself: who am I to start doing these projects for myself, when I've got so many other things I have to do for others?

You might start to wonder what others are going to think about your new venture. What are they going to say? Your friends might get jealous when you start to enjoy the fruits of your labor, be it produce from a garden plot, newly painted designs in your bathroom that you designed and stenciled yourself, or your success in changing your  bike tube and tire. They might envy the exhilaration you exhibit when you show them the embroidered pillow project you completed or the bars of soap that you made. Instead of going to Pier One or Pottery Barn to decorate your home, you've actually made something that you wrought, something that you directly made, by your hand.

There is little to compare with the upwelling of personal power and strength you will feel when you complete your project and consider it your personal success. What a feeling for you when what you believed you could do became what you actually did! There will be a cascade of positive effects for your self-sustaining future, as you consider your newfound sense of self-reliance and self-confidence. Being able to post your pics and your success on your social media accounts is going to be so much fun! You've created something of value for yourself that you might choose to share with others.

Honor Your Belief in the Project

Your successful efforts on your small project are a metaphor for your advances in reclaiming your sense of self-reliance amid the blizzard of distractions and cross-currents in your life that diminish your focus. Again, your belief in your future creative success can be predicted from your success in past efforts. Recall the smaller instances where you believed that you could create change on a small scale; you did it, and now you might consider a larger opportunity to explore and succeed. You're traveling a creative path that others have taken before you.

◆ ◆ ◆

*With your effort you share the same path of others
on the creative journey.*

◆ ◆ ◆

For the chair, I became intrigued by an Arts And Crafts ideal that the method of construction is reflected in the work; be it back assembly adjustment pegs, exposed pegged joinery or evidence of controlled hammer blows across a copper surface.

If you've become interested in wheel thrown pottery, you are following in a tradition of other potters who shape the clay and bring forth similar shapes. All have struggled and succeeded, in exciting steps forward and sudden stops to reconsider a new path or technique. Everyone starts at the beginning with belief. If you've taken up metalworking, you will follow in the same footsteps as the others who have applied their hammer to metal to shape it in similar ways.

I'd ask you to keep your desired goal before you all the time. It is encouraging when your effort begins to match your imagined goal for

yourself. Your belief in your final attainment can become motivation if you have a series of setbacks or have made bad choices.

During the creative working time, I'd recommend maintaining your methodical pace through to the end. However, as you approach your end, you might become eager for completion. Plan to wait. If you are patching a masonry wall or laying down a vinyl tile floor, the time of curing for the cement is outside your control. Budget in and honor that time before foot traffic is allowed to cross. Avoid being rushed on your final processes. Don't scrap all your hard work that you've done with a rash judgment to shortcuts that jeopardize your end result.

Believe that you are creating something that furthers your interest; that builds to something in the future. In some cases, what you are creating will have a life beyond your own. What you create now may be the way that you are remembered to others or to the future.

Honor Your Belief in the Outcome

Where you put your time and energy is important. If you are committed to the effort, you will not want a mediocre result. Respect the outcome from the beginning steps. From those beginning steps know that consistent, directed effort and intention over an extended period of time will bring you to your goal. This has happened for those before you and this will be the same for you. Know that you will complete to a standard that reflects your intentions for a good outcome.

◆ ◆ ◆

You have what you need to start. Your creative effort is a bequest of your humanity. Remain curious about the outcome.

◆ ◆ ◆

For the Morris Chair, I became interested in the balance between precise enough and good enough. During the time away from the shop, I realized that my precision, as best I could in the early stages would determine my personal satisfaction to the future. Much like a billiard ball on the way to the pocket, must roll correctly from the start, if I impatiently cut the shoulders of the tenon before assembly, I would regret it months later with a sloppy fit at the tenon shoulder.

For your creative effort, manage your tools and your materials with the expectation of an eventual successful outcome.

Adopt a realistic goal and consider the path. Take on projects that reflect your experience and your accumulated skills, while adopting the belief that you will learn and know more as you proceed. However don't wait to start until all is in place before making a first step. Prepare for what you know will be needed for a first milestone on the journey. Make realistic judgments of the time available, your latent abilities, your newly accumulated skills and make those steps toward your desired goal. And then move with confidence toward the start, as you carry a vision of completion as your motivation.

What Have I Learned About Belief from the Morris Chair?

○ As a novice, start on small projects, with short completion times or lesser difficulty. Gain confidence and experience in the simple before attempting the complex. You deserve to be successful in your effort. It feels good to make your own stuff. Give yourself permission. Allow yourself to explore your maker self. This is what you wanted to do.

○ A creative outlook is a component of your humanity. It is right that you are returning to a creative, problem solving and hand wrought solution to your self-sufficiency. You follow in a proud tradition of self-reliance and ingenuity like those before you. Take the time necessary for a satisfying outcome.

● Commit to a high standard for yourself. Don't wait until all is perfect to begin. Assemble what you need to start for a reasonable mid-project outcome; refresh and resume. Assess needs, acquire tools, material and knowledge, then take action on your worthy goal.

Insight Collection

Metamorphosis

What you change about yourself might change the way that other people perceive you.

Carefully balance your actual and imagined skills with the emerging challenge before you.

For your personal safety and best project outcomes, respect the tools, materials and procedures that you will use to explore your DIY creative interests.

Overcoming Fear

In facing fear, recall your successful past to pave your future.

Generally you are your own worst critic.

Follow your curiosity, assess your skills, begin your effort as you can without judgment.

Letting Go

Advice and plans are only a guide for your creative expression.

Use the knowledge you have and ask for the knowledge you have not. Then step forward.

Aim for perfection, settle for the best.

Best Choice, Bad Choices

Recover, re-commit and re-start after a bad choice.

As you explore more of your creative expression, expect to continue to be surprised.

Repeat the best choices. Recover from the poor choices. Retreat, re-focus, resume.

Belief

This is your choice to do as you want, to feel accomplished in what you do, to see your creative exploration as another avenue to knowing yourself.

With your effort, you share the same path of others on the creative journey.

You have what you need to start. Your creative effort is a bequest of your humanity. Remain curious about the outcome.

Epilogue

Quite obviously, the building of my Morris Chair in 1999-2000 became much more to me than simply the assembly of carefully sawn pieces of wood arranged in a predetermined pattern. Quite obviously, I learned a lot about myself through this effort.

I learned that I can meet or exceed my expectations of myself. I learned that I can create an object of lasting beauty and value for myself. I learned that I enjoy watching others enjoy the results of my efforts.

I hope that you can learn resilience, improve your self-esteem, self-reliance and internal strength all the while you are challenged by the creative process.

It is my fervent wish through the writing of this book that I have inspired you to consider your creative potential to change the way that you see yourself in your world. That you will use your head, heart and hands to surprise yourself and delight others with what you can do with your creative human birthright.

◆ ◆ ◆

On September 21, 2010, fully ten years after I completed the Morris Chair, I was asked by Oscar Fitzgerald, furniture curator at the Smithsonian Institution to demonstrate my chair for a class of the Corcoran School of Art-Decorative Arts Masters Program. My talk was titled "Methods and Motivations in Arts and Crafts Furniture Construction."

◆ ◆ ◆

For More Information

If, after reading my book, you have become inspired to explore your creative life to start making your own things for yourself or for others, please contact me on my Facebook page "Awaken Creative Potential", via Twitter @zenmorrischair or through my web page at *www.awakencreativepotential.com.*

I'd like to hear from you about how you are exploring your creative effort.

◆ ◆ ◆

About the Author

Randy Gafner has been associated with the makers movement for decades. He feels that creative process and action breeds self-reliance and self-expression which leads to more fulfillment and higher quality of life. He thinks that in this post-modern era everyone would benefit by making more of their own things using their ideas, skills, and abilities drawn from across the creative spectrum.

Gafner has worked for over 25 years as a national and international video-journalist and communications professional. He is a skilled jazz musician, a proficient craftsman and an eager world traveller. Ever the inveterate life long learner, he recently completed a MA degree in Health Communication from George Mason University in Fairfax, Virginia.

◆ ◆ ◆

Footnotes

1. Fumed oak- an atmospheric wood finish technique involving deliberate exposure of oak to high concentrations of aqueous ammonia fumes (>29%). The ammonia chemically reacts with the naturally occurring tannins in the oak; the wood darkens.

2. Ray Flake-the wood grain feature revealed by rift or quarter-sawing an oak log. The ray flake of the finished lumber is the cross-section of the more dense medullary ray of the log.

3. The singular post of the floor lamp and then later the four quadralinear legs of the Morris Chair have the same joinery construction. The boards of post/legs are mitered at a 45 degree angle and glued together at the corners to form a hollow column with the visually desirable face grain showing on all 4 sides.

◆ ◆ ◆

Thanks for following my journey with the chair. I hope that you realize that my story is not about the successful completion of the project that I took on but is rather about the lessons I learned. I hope to offer encouragement for you to consider your creative path.

In current times of advancing automation and emerging technology it is so easy to overlook the human need of hand built creativity for benefit in our daily lives. From my story you know how Awakening Creativity will ignite your passion for living. You can see how everyday tasks can become the mindful catalyst for you to discover your maker avatar and to unleash creativity in your life. This is a way to reshape and enhance your life direction.

I am already hard at work in my next book Awaken Creative Potential, which is filled with inspiring scientific research and personal stories from my readers about how their personal creativity and intention dramatically connect them to a more centered lifestyle.

For now, my personal challenge for you is to open your life to allow more personal creativity. I give you my permission for that exploration. I've set aside some space below, right here, right now, just for you to design your own creative awakening...

I want to learn about what you've done. I love hearing about your breakthroughs. Please visit my community at **www.awakencreativepotential.com** and share your story.

Randy

Awaken
Creative
Potential

Below is an outline for your own creative dream :

Perhaps you've been inspired to make something?

What would you make?

How might you make time, a little every day?

What are you afraid of?

What could happen for you?

What do you currently believe about your maker potential?